Puddings

Alex Barker

TESCO

About the author

Alex Barker has written numerous books and articles on food and has been the cookery editor of several leading women's magazines. She now lives in the country, where she tries out all her new ideas on her very willing family.

Photographer	Thomas Odulate
Home economist	Lucy McKelvie
Stylist	Antonia Gaunt
Recipes tested by	Terry Farris

CONTENTS

INTRODUCTION

The recipes in this book have been created and photographed specially for Tesco. They have been thoroughly tested and all the ingredients are normally available at larger Tesco stores, when in season. There is no need for any special kitchen equipment.

Using the recipes

1 Both metric and imperial weights and measures are given, except for goods sold in standard size packaging, such as cans. As conversions are not always exact, you should follow either the metric or the imperial throughout each recipe where possible.

2 British standard level spoon measurements are used throughout. A tablespoon measure is equivalent to 15ml; a teaspoon is equivalent to 5ml.

3 Dishes cooked in the oven should be placed in the centre, unless otherwise stated.

4 Tesco advises that all eggs should be cooked thoroughly. Where the cooking time is not sufficiently long, dried egg has been used.

5 Some of the recipes in this book include nuts. These should not be eaten by children, people who have an allergic reaction to nuts, or women who are pregnant or breastfeeding. It is advisable to check the labelling of any commercially prepared products to ensure that they do not contain nuts or nut derivatives. Recipes including honey should not be eaten by children under the age of 12 months.

6 Fruits are medium-sized, unless otherwise stated. If cooking or serving fruits with their skins on, make sure they are thoroughly washed.

7 The fat and calorie content of each recipe is given. These figures are for one serving only.

8 Each recipe has a simplicity rating of 1, 2 or 3 chef's hats. Recipes with 1 hat are easy; those with 2 or 3 will require a little more effort.

BROWN BREAD AND MINT ICE CREAM

Serves 4

Preparation 15 mins
plus 20 mins cooling and
2 hrs freezing

Cooking 5 mins

Calories 493

Fat 33g

Simplicity

1 Heat the butter in a saucepan until melted, then add the sugar and breadcrumbs. Cook gently for 3-4 minutes, stirring, until the breadcrumbs are slightly golden and crisp. Stir in the chopped mint, then leave to cool for 20 minutes.

2 Whip the cream until it forms soft peaks, then fold in the breadcrumb mixture and the custard. Spoon into a freezer container and freeze for 2 hours. Serve in scoops decorated with the mint leaves.

50g (2oz) butter

50g (2oz) demerara sugar

175g (6oz) fresh wholemeal breadcrumbs

2 tbsp finely chopped fresh mint, plus extra leaves to decorate

200ml (7fl oz) whipping or double cream

200ml (7fl oz) ready-made custard

If you've never tried brown bread ice cream, you've been missing out! It's at its best when it's still creamy and the breadcrumbs are crisp. If you make it a day in advance, soften it in the fridge for 30 minutes before serving.

WARM APRICOT BRIOCHES

Simplicity

Serves 4

Preparation 10 mins

Cooking 8 mins

Calories 226

Fat 6g

4 individual brioches

6 fresh apricots, halved and stoned, or 12 canned apricot halves, drained

6 tbsp apricot conserve or jam

1 tbsp orange juice

4 small scoops vanilla ice cream

1 Preheat the oven to 180°C/350°F/Gas Mark 4. Slice the top off each brioche and reserve, then carefully hollow out the centres and discard. Place 3 apricot halves in the middle of each brioche.

2 Put the brioches and their tops onto a baking sheet and cook for 8 minutes or until heated through and slightly crispy. Meanwhile, gently heat the conserve or jam in a saucepan with the orange juice, stirring, until melted.

3 Place each brioche on a plate and top with a scoop of ice cream. Drizzle the conserve or jam mixture over, then replace the tops.

For speed, looks and taste, this pudding is hard to beat. It's also versatile: try using crème fraîche instead of ice cream, and quartered peaches rather than apricots.

GLAZED APPLES IN BRANDY SNAP BASKETS

Serves 6

Preparation 10 mins

Cooking 5 mins

Calories 217

Fat 14g

Simplicity

1 Place the apples in a saucepan with the butter, sugar and brandy or Calvados, if using. Simmer for 5 minutes or until the apples have softened.

2 Mix together the lemon curd and crème fraîche, then divide between the brandy snap baskets. Spoon the apple mixture over, decorate with the lemon rind and serve straight away.

2 large eating apples, peeled, cored and thickly sliced

25g (1oz) butter

1 tbsp caster sugar

2 tbsp brandy or Calvados (optional)

2 tbsp lemon curd

125ml (4½fl oz) crème fraîche

6 brandy snap baskets

Thin strips lemon rind, pared with a vegetable peeler, to decorate

Ready-made brandy snap baskets make this really quick to prepare – but who'd guess? The apples can be cooked a few hours in advance and reheated at the last moment.

HONEYED FIGS WITH MASCARPONE

Simplicity

Serves 4

Preparation 10 mins

Cooking 10 mins

Calories 228

Fat 15g

12-16 fresh figs, depending on their size

2 tbsp clear honey

1 tbsp pine nut kernels

100g (3½oz) mascarpone

1 Preheat the oven to 180°C/350°F/Gas Mark 4. Cut a deep cross into each fig at the stalk end, then open out slightly. Place the figs close together in an ovenproof dish to keep them upright.

2 Drizzle the honey over and inside the figs, then cook for 10 minutes, until soft. Meanwhile, place a frying pan over a medium heat and dry-fry the pine nuts for 2 minutes, until golden, stirring often.

3 Transfer 3-4 figs to each serving plate, scatter the pine nuts around them and serve with a spoonful of mascarpone.

Luscious figs and creamy mascarpone are the perfect end to any meal. Only use ripe fresh figs for this Italian pudding – canned ones are too soft and sweet.

STRAWBERRY TRIFLE BRULEE

Serves 4

Preparation 15 mins

plus 2 hrs chilling

Cooking 3 mins

Calories 236

Fat 11g

Simplicity

1 Divide the biscuits or sponge halves between 4 x 150ml (¼ pint) ramekins and spoon over the Madeira, sherry or kirsch.

2 Whip the cream until it forms soft peaks, then fold in the custard and strawberries. Divide the cream mixture between the ramekins. Smooth the tops and sprinkle over a thick layer of sugar.

3 Meanwhile, preheat the grill to high. Place the ramekins under the grill for 2-3 minutes, until the sugar caramelises. Leave to cool, then refrigerate for 2 hours before serving.

75g (3oz) amaretti biscuits, roughly crushed, or 2 trifle sponges, cut in half

2 tbsp Madeira, sweet sherry or kirsch

75ml (3fl oz) whipping or double cream

75ml (3fl oz) ready-made custard

100g (3½oz) strawberries, hulled and halved

3 tbsp demerara sugar

...strawberries and crushed almond biscuits in a light, creamy custard, covered by a layer of caramelised sugar – it's easy and tastes every bit as good as it sounds.

CHEAT'S KEY LIME PIE

Simplicity

Serves 6

Preparation 25 mins

plus 1 hr chilling

Cooking 4 mins

Calories 241

Fat 12g

75ml (3fl oz) whipping or double cream

150ml (¼ pint) condensed milk

Grated rind and juice of 2 limes

18cm (7in) sweet pastry case

275g pack meringue mix

1 Whip the cream until it forms soft peaks. Gently fold in the condensed milk, lime rind and juice. Spoon the mixture into the pastry case and place in the fridge for 1 hour – the mixture is quite loose at first but firms up when refrigerated.

2 Meanwhile, make the meringue topping according to the packet instructions, whisking until it forms stiff peaks (this is best done with an electric whisk).

3 Preheat the grill to medium. Spoon the meringue over the cream mixture. Grill for 2-4 minutes, until the meringue turns golden. Serve either warm or cold.

This tangy alternative to lemon meringue pie comes from the Florida Keys. It's still on the menus of many of the seafront cafés. One bite, and you'll think you're there!

PASSION FRUIT AND MANGO GRANITA

Serves 4

Preparation 25 mins
plus 20 mins cooling and
3 hrs freezing

Cooking 5 mins

Calories 92

Fat trace

Simplicity

2 passion fruit

300ml (½ pint) fresh
orange juice

Juice of 1 lemon

2 tbsp clear honey

1 ripe mango

1 Halve the passion fruit, then scoop out the pulp and seeds and place in a small saucepan with the orange and lemon juice and honey. Bring to the boil and cook for 1 minute, stirring, or until the honey dissolves. Leave to cool for 20 minutes.

2 Peel the mango and cut off 8 thin slices. Wrap them in cling film and place in the fridge. Chop the remaining mango flesh and blend with the passion fruit mixture in a food processor or using a hand blender – the mixture should be fairly smooth but the seeds should remain whole.

3 Pour into a freezer container and freeze for 2 hours, whisking once or twice to break up any large ice crystals, then freeze for a further 1 hour or until the mixture crystallises. Serve the granita in small glasses, each one topped with 2 mango slices.

This tropical alternative to ice cream is perfect in summer.
You can make it a few days in advance, but defrost it for
15 minutes and then break it up with a fork before eating.

CITRUS FRUIT SALAD WITH GINGER

Simplicity

Serves 4	**Calories** 96
Preparation 20 mins	**Fat** trace
Cooking 15 mins	

1 pink grapefruit

1 large orange

1 tangerine, peeled and divided into segments

Rind of 1 lime, pared with a vegetable peeler and cut into matchsticks

50g (2oz) kumquats, halved and pips removed

Juice of 1 small lemon

150ml (¼ pint) ginger beer

3 tbsp caster sugar

2 pieces stem ginger in syrup, drained and finely chopped

Fresh mint to decorate

1 Slice the tops and bottoms off the grapefruit and orange, using a sharp, serrated knife. Cut down the side of the fruits, following the curves, to remove the skin and pith. Hold the fruit over a bowl to catch the juices and cut out the segments, leaving the membranes behind. Place in a serving dish with the tangerine segments. Reserve the fruit juices.

2 Place the lime rind and kumquats in a saucepan with 150ml (¼ pint) of water. Simmer for 10 minutes or until softened. Add the kumquats to the other fruit and drain the lime rind on kitchen towels. Reserve the liquid.

3 Add the lemon juice, ginger beer, sugar and any juices from the fruit to the reserved cooking liquid. Heat gently, stirring, for 5 minutes or until the sugar dissolves. Pour the mixture over the fruit and stir in the chopped ginger. Sprinkle over the lime rind and the fresh mint.

You can use whichever citrus fruits you like in this dessert, but don't leave out the lime – its flavour and colour make all the difference to this fruit salad.

GRILLED PEACHES WITH FROMAGE FRAIS

Serves 4

Preparation 5 mins

Cooking 7 mins

Calories 164

Fat 6g

Simplicity

1 Cut each peach in half from top to bottom and, using both hands, twist to loosen the flesh from the stone. Carefully remove the stone with the point of a knife.

2 Place the peach halves, cut-side up, in a shallow flameproof dish. Divide the amaretti biscuits between the peach halves and top each with a large spoonful of fromage frais.

3 Preheat the grill to medium. Grill the peaches for 5 minutes or until the tops are lightly browned, then sprinkle with a little sugar. Increase the heat and grill for another 2 minutes or until the sugar browns slightly.

6 ripe peaches

50g (2oz) amaretti biscuits, roughly crushed

200g (7oz) low-fat fromage frais

1 tbsp caster sugar

Don't worry if you don't have any ripe peaches – use canned ones instead, and this pudding will still be a hit. You can also swap the fromage frais for mascarpone.

MIXED FRUIT COMPOTE

Simplicity

Serves 4

Preparation 10 mins

Cooking 30 mins

Calories 235

Fat trace

225g (8oz) fresh rhubarb, chopped

50g (2oz) soft light brown sugar

400g (14oz) mixed ready-to-eat dried fruit, such as apricots, peaches, apples and pears, cut into even-sized pieces

1 Preheat the oven to 180°C/350°F/Gas Mark 4. Place the rhubarb in a saucepan with the sugar and 300ml (½ pint) water. Simmer for 5 minutes or until the fruit begins to soften.

2 Place the dried fruit in an ovenproof dish, add the rhubarb and its cooking liquid and stir gently.

3 Cover the dish and bake for 20-25 minutes, stirring halfway through cooking, until the fruit has softened. Serve warm or chilled.

This pudding is so healthy that you may want to have it for breakfast too! It's delicious served with a little honey and natural yogurt or crème fraîche – at any time of day.

BAKED SPICED PEARS

Serves 4

Preparation 10 mins

Cooking 30 mins

Calories 120

Fat 5g

Simplicity

1 Preheat the oven to 230°C/450°F/Gas Mark 8. Place the lemon juice, butter, honey, cardamom, cinnamon and caraway seeds in a small saucepan. Stir to combine, then heat gently for 10 minutes to allow the flavours to develop.

2 Place the pears, flat-side down, in an ovenproof dish. Pour the lemon juice mixture over the pears, discarding the cardamom pods and cinnamon sticks, if using. Bake for 20 minutes or until the pears are soft, spooning over the juices halfway through. Serve hot, with any juices spooned over the top.

Juice of 1 lemon
25g (1oz) butter
3 tbsp clear honey
5 cardamom pods, split
2 sticks cinnamon or ½ tsp ground cinnamon
½ tsp caraway seeds
4 small, firm Conference pears, peeled, halved and cored

The spices combine with the natural sweetness of the pears to create a great ending to a heavy meal. Serve with low-fat yogurt, cream or a dollop of crème fraîche.

CREAMY RASPBERRY FOOL

Simplicity

Serves 4

Preparation 10 mins
plus 2-3 hrs chilling

Calories 215

Fat 20g

300g (11oz) fresh raspberries

50g (2oz) caster sugar

200ml carton crème fraîche

1 Reserve a few raspberries for decoration, then mix the rest with 25g (1oz) of the sugar and press the mixture through a sieve. Stir in the remaining sugar to taste.

2 Place the crème fraîche in a large bowl and gently fold in the raspberry purée until combined. Spoon into small coffee cups or glasses and refrigerate for 2-3 hours to firm up slightly. Serve decorated with the reserved raspberries.

This fool is so simple to make, yet it's special enough to serve at any dinner party. Don't put the raspberries on top too far in advance – they might start to sink.

SUMMER PUDDING WITH REDCURRANT SAUCE

Serves 6

Preparation 20 mins

plus 2-3 hrs chilling

Cooking 8 mins

Calories 177

Fat trace

Simplicity

1 Place the fruit, sugar and 3 tablespoons of water in a saucepan and simmer for 5 minutes or until the fruit has softened. Leave to cool slightly.

2 Line the base and sides of a 900ml (1½ pint) pudding basin with 6 slices of the bread, cutting to fit and making sure there are no gaps. Strain the fruit, reserving the juice, then add the fruit to the basin. Cover with the remaining bread to form a lid. Spoon over 3-4 tablespoons of the reserved juice.

3 Place a plate on top of the bread, with a weight, such as a large can, on it. Place in the fridge for 2-3 hours to let the juices soak through the bread.

4 For the sauce, strain the reserved juice into a pan, then add the redcurrant jelly. Simmer for 2-3 minutes, stirring, until the jelly has melted. Invert the pudding onto a plate and serve with the redcurrant sauce.

1kg (2lb 4oz) fresh or frozen mixed berry fruits

3 tbsp caster sugar

8 slices white or wholemeal bread, crusts removed

2 tbsp redcurrant jelly

This is many people's favourite pudding – it's easy to make and healthy too. However, it just wouldn't taste the same without at least a spoonful of whipped cream.

THREE BERRY FRUIT SALAD WITH PASTRY TWISTS

Simplicity

Serves 4

Preparation 20 mins
plus 1 hr chilling

Cooking time 10 mins

Calories 305

Fat 11g

500g (1lb 2oz) mixed fresh strawberries, raspberries and blackberries

3 tbsp caster sugar

150ml (¼ pint) red or rosé wine

For the pastry twists

Butter for greasing

175g (6oz) ready-rolled puff pastry, defrosted if frozen

2 tbsp caster sugar

1 tsp ground cinnamon

1 Halve the strawberries. Place all the fruit in a bowl and sprinkle over the caster sugar. Stir in the wine and mix thoroughly. Cover and place in the fridge for 1 hour to allow the flavours to develop.

2 Preheat the oven to 220°C/425°F/Gas Mark 7. Lightly grease a baking sheet. To make the pastry twists, lay the pastry on a floured board and sprinkle with ½ tablespoon of the sugar and ½ teaspoon of the cinnamon. Roll out slightly and fold in half, then sprinkle with another ½ tablespoon of sugar and the remaining cinnamon. Cut into 2.5cm (1in) wide strips and carefully twist each one.

3 Place the twists on the baking sheet and sprinkle with the remaining sugar. Cook for 10 minutes or until golden. Serve with the fruit salad.

A little wine turns a straight fruit salad into something much more decadent and exciting. But if you don't want to make it alcoholic, use cranberry juice instead.

STRAWBERRY AND CREAM TARTLETS

Serves 4

Preparation 25 mins
plus 15 mins chilling and
15 mins cooling

Cooking 20 mins

Calories 549

Fat 38g

Simplicity

1 Preheat the oven to 190°C/375°F/Gas Mark 5. Sift the flour and sugar into a bowl. Rub in the butter and the lemon juice and knead lightly until the mixture forms a smooth dough. Cover with cling film and refrigerate for 15 minutes.

2 Roll the dough out thinly on a lightly floured surface, divide into 4 and use to line 4 x 7.5cm (3in) loose-bottomed tartlet tins. Line with baking paper and baking beans and bake for 15 minutes. Remove the paper and beans and cook for another 3-5 minutes, until the pastry is golden. Leave to cool for 15 minutes, then remove from the tins.

3 Whip the cream with the lemon rind until it forms soft peaks. Spoon into the cases and top with the strawberries. Melt the jam or jelly over a gentle heat with 1 tablespoon of water, then press through a sieve and cool slightly. Spoon over the strawberries, then dust with icing sugar.

150g (5oz) plain flour
20g (¾oz) icing sugar, plus extra to dust
100g (3½oz) unsalted butter, softened
Finely grated rind of 1 small lemon, plus 1 tsp juice
142ml carton double or whipping cream
225g (8oz) strawberries, halved
4 tbsp raspberry jam or redcurrant jelly to glaze

You can fill these light pastry cases with virtually any fruit you like. Grapes, cherries or raspberries are all delicious – simply vary the jam to suit whatever you use.

BLACKCURRANT AND LEMON SOUFFLES

Simplicity

Serves 4

Preparation 20 mins

Cooking 35 mins

Calories 233

Fat 18g

175g (6oz) blackcurrants

100g (3½oz) caster sugar

1 tbsp cassis or other fruit liqueur

50g (2oz) butter, softened, plus extra for greasing

Finely grated rind and juice of 1 lemon

3 medium eggs, separated

100g (3½oz) cream cheese

Icing sugar to dust

1 Preheat the oven to 190°C/375°F/Gas Mark 5. Place the blackcurrants in a small saucepan with 50g (2oz) of the sugar and cook for 3 minutes or until they begin to split. Stir in the cassis or other fruit liqueur, then set aside. Lightly grease 4 x 150ml (¼ pint) ramekins with butter.

2 Beat the butter with the remaining sugar until pale and creamy. Beat in the lemon rind and juice, egg yolks and cream cheese. Whisk the egg whites until they form stiff peaks (this is best done with an electric whisk). Carefully fold a spoonful of the egg whites into the cream cheese mixture to loosen, then fold in the rest.

3 Divide the blackcurrant mixture between the ramekins and top with the cream cheese mixture. Bake for 30 minutes or until risen and firm. Dust the soufflés with icing sugar and serve straight away.

Hidden under this feather-light lemon soufflé is a layer of juicy blackcurrants. The fruit can get really hot so make sure you warn everyone not to burn their mouths.

RED FRUIT AND CUSTARD FILO PARCELS

Serves 4

Preparation 15 mins

Cooking 10 mins

Calories 354

Fat 7g

Simplicity

1 Preheat the oven to 220°C/425°F/Gas Mark 7. Lightly grease a baking sheet. Brush 3 half-sheets of pastry with the melted butter. Stack them on top of each other, buttered-sides up, then place an unbuttered half on top. Repeat with the remaining pastry sheets to make 4 wrappings for the parcels.

2 Mix the raspberries and blackberries with the brown sugar. Spoon 1 tablespoon of custard on top of each pastry stack and brush the edges with butter. Top the custard with a little fruit mixture and gather in the pastry sides, squeezing together to seal. Place on the baking sheet, brush with the remaining butter and cook for 7-10 minutes, until golden.

3 To make the fruit sauce, press the fruit through a sieve and stir in the sugar to taste. Place the parcels on plates and spoon around the sauce. Decorate with the fresh raspberries or blackberries and dust with icing sugar.

8 large sheets fresh filo pastry, cut in half

25g (1oz) butter, melted, plus extra for greasing

50g (2oz) each of fresh raspberries and blackberries

½ tbsp soft light brown sugar

4 tbsp ready-made custard

Fresh raspberries or blackberries to decorate and icing sugar to dust

For the fruit sauce

50g (2oz) each of fresh raspberries and blackberries

1 tbsp caster sugar

These little golden parcels have a fabulous range of textures – crisp filo pastry, soft fruit and creamy custard. If you want, you can add a spoonful of Greek yogurt too.

LEMON AND CINNAMON EVE'S PUDDING

Simplicity

Serves 4

Preparation 20 mins

Cooking time 35 mins

Calories 453

Fat 24g

450g (1lb) cooking apples, peeled, cored and chopped

100g (3½oz) caster sugar

½ tsp ground cinnamon

100g (3½oz) soft margarine

Finely grated rind of 1 lemon and juice of ½ lemon

2 medium eggs, lightly beaten

100g (3½oz) self-raising flour, sifted

1 Preheat the oven to 180°C/350°F/Gas Mark 4. Place the apples in a saucepan with 2 tablespoons of the sugar and 1 tablespoon of water. Cover and cook over a low heat for 3-4 minutes, until the apples begin to soften, then add the cinnamon and stir. Transfer to a 23 x 15cm (9 x 6in) ovenproof dish.

2 Beat the margarine and the remaining sugar until pale and creamy, then add the lemon rind and juice, the eggs and flour. Beat the mixture to a soft, dropping consistency.

3 Spoon the mixture over the apples, smooth with the back of a spoon, and bake for 25-30 minutes, until well risen, golden and just firm to the touch.

Often the best recipes are the old-fashioned ones. In this comforting pudding, a lemony sponge covers cinnamon-scented apples. Cream goes with it perfectly.

DATE PUDDINGS WITH STICKY TOFFEE SAUCE

Serves 4

Preparation 20 mins
plus 10 mins soaking and
5 mins cooling

Cooking 25 mins

Calories 633

Fat 32g

Simplicity

1 Preheat the oven to 180°C/350°F/Gas Mark 4. Grease 4 x 200ml (7fl oz) pudding basins or ramekins with butter. Cover the dates with boiling water and soak for 10 minutes to soften.

2 Beat the butter, sugar and vanilla essence until pale and creamy. Beat in the eggs, then fold in the flour and baking powder. Strain the dates and blend to a purée in a food processor, or mash with a fork. Stir into the mixture with the banana.

3 Spoon the mixture into the basins or ramekins, almost to their tops, and place on a baking sheet. Bake for 20 minutes or until well risen and just firm to the touch. Cool for 5 minutes, then loosen the puddings with a knife and invert onto plates.

4 To make the sauce, place the sugar, butter and cream in a pan and heat gently for 5 minutes or until syrupy. Pour over the puddings to serve.

75g (3oz) butter, softened, plus extra for greasing

100g (3½oz) stoned dates, chopped

100g (3½oz) soft light brown sugar

½ tsp vanilla essence

2 large eggs

100g (3½oz) plain wholemeal flour

1½ tsp baking powder

1 very ripe banana, mashed

For the toffee sauce

75g (3oz) soft dark brown sugar

50g (2oz) butter

2 tbsp single cream

Sponge pudding, bananas, dates, and a sticky toffee sauce...what a great combination! You can serve it on its own or with a big scoop of good vanilla ice cream.

CARAMELISED BANANA PANCAKES

Simplicity 👨‍🍳👨‍🍳

Serves 4

Preparation 10 mins

Cooking 25 mins

Calories 250

Fat 10g

1 large egg
100g (3½oz) plain flour, sifted
Pinch of salt
250ml (9fl oz) half-fat milk
25g (1oz) butter, melted
Sunflower oil for greasing
2 large, firm bananas, sliced
3 tbsp Madeira, dessert wine or 2 tbsp Drambuie
2-3 tsp demerara sugar

1 Beat the egg, flour, salt and a little milk to a smooth paste. Gradually mix in the remaining milk, then stir in the melted butter.

2 Brush a non-stick, medium-sized frying pan with the oil and heat until very hot. Pour in 2-3 tablespoons of batter, swirling to cover the base of the pan. Cook the pancakes for 1-2 minutes on each side, until golden. Repeat to make 7 more, keeping the pancakes warm and layering them between sheets of baking paper to stop them sticking.

3 Preheat the grill to high. Wipe the pan, add the bananas and Madeira, wine or Drambuie and heat through gently, stirring.

4 When most of the liquid has evaporated, place a spoonful of the banana mixture on each pancake, fold it into quarters and place in a flameproof dish. Sprinkle with the sugar and grill until the tops of the pancakes are golden and lightly caramelised.

These pancakes filled with hot gooey bananas have a hidden kick! For children, you can replace the alcohol with maple syrup. Serve with Greek yogurt or ice cream.

RHUBARB AND APPLE OATY CRUMBLE

Serves 4

Preparation 20 mins

Cooking time 50 mins

Calories 312

Fat 12g

Simplicity

1 Preheat the oven to 180°C/350°F/Gas Mark 4. Place the rhubarb, orange juice and sugar in a saucepan. Cover and cook for 4-5 minutes, until the rhubarb begins to soften. Place the mixture in a lightly greased 23 x 15cm (9 x 6in) ovenproof dish, then stir in the apples.

2 To make the crumble, rub the butter or margarine into the flour with your fingertips, until the mixture resembles coarse breadcrumbs. Mix in the oats and sugar, then sprinkle over the fruit mixture. Bake for 40-45 minutes, until the topping is crisp and golden.

225g (8oz) rhubarb, chopped

2 tbsp fresh orange juice

2 tbsp sugar or to taste

Butter for greasing

225g (8oz) eating apples, cored and chopped

For the crumble

50g (2oz) chilled butter or block margarine, cubed

75g (3oz) plain wholemeal flour

50g (2oz) porridge oats

50g (2oz) soft light brown sugar

Dark sugar and oats give this topping a fuller flavour and chewier texture than ordinary crumble. It's good with cream – especially if you stir in some grated orange rind.

PEAR AND ALMOND FLAN

Simplicity 🍳 🍳

Serves 6

Preparation 20 mins
plus 10 mins chilling and
15 mins cooling

Cooking 50 mins

Calories 419

Fat 26g

2 large, firm pears, peeled, cored and sliced

1 tsp lemon juice

50g (2oz) caster sugar

200g (7oz) shortcrust pastry, defrosted if frozen

3-4 tbsp apricot or plum jam

50g (2oz) soft margarine

1 medium egg

50g (2oz) self-raising flour

50g (2oz) ground almonds

25g (1oz) flaked almonds

Icing sugar to dust

1 Preheat the oven to 190°C/375°F/Gas Mark 5. Toss the pears with the lemon juice and 1 teaspoon of the caster sugar.

2 Roll the pastry out thinly on a lightly floured surface and line a 20cm (8in) loose-bottomed flan tin. Refrigerate for 10 minutes. Line the pastry with baking paper and a layer of baking beans and cook for 15 minutes. Remove the paper and beans and cook for another 5 minutes or until lightly golden. Leave to cool for 5 minutes.

3 Spread the jam over the pastry and top with the pears. Beat the margarine and remaining sugar until pale and creamy, then add the egg, flour and ground almonds and beat to a soft, dropping consistency. Spoon the mixture over the pears, sprinkle with flaked almonds and cook for 30 minutes or until set and golden. Cool for 10 minutes, then transfer to a plate and dust with icing sugar.

Hidden in the middle of this sophisticated pudding is a layer of jam, which makes it sweeter and even more delicious. Serve with a little cream or crème fraîche.

BLUEBERRY AND ORANGE CLAFOUTIS

Serves 4

Preparation 10 mins

plus 5 mins cooling

Cooking 40 mins

Calories 346

Fat 20g

Simplicity

1 Preheat the oven to 190°C/375°F/Gas Mark 5. Grease a shallow 20cm (8in) ovenproof dish with butter, then spoon in the blueberries.

2 Place the eggs, sugar, vanilla essence, orange rind and juice and the flour in a bowl, then beat until smooth. Gently stir in the soured cream and melted butter, then pour the mixture over the blueberries. Bake for 40 minutes or until risen and set. Cool for 5 minutes, then dust with icing sugar.

40g (1½oz) butter, melted, plus extra for greasing

200g (7oz) blueberries

3 medium eggs

75g (3oz) caster sugar

Few drops vanilla essence

Finely grated rind and juice of ½ orange

50g (2oz) plain flour, sifted

142ml carton soured cream

Icing sugar to dust

This light batter pudding is much easier to make than it looks. You can use all sorts of other fruits instead of blueberries, but dark red cherries are particularly good.

PLUM TART WITH CRUMBLE TOPPING

Simplicity 🧑‍🍳 🧑‍🍳

Serves 6

Preparation 15 mins
plus 10 mins chilling and
5 mins cooling

Cooking 35 mins

Calories 296

Fat 15g

200g (7oz) shortcrust pastry,
defrosted if frozen

400g (14oz) plums or damsons,
halved and stoned

3 tbsp caster sugar

1 tsp cornflour

50g (2oz) chopped mixed nuts

2 tbsp demerara sugar

2 tbsp fresh breadcrumbs

1 Preheat the oven to 190°C/375°F/Gas Mark 5. Roll the pastry out thinly on a lightly floured surface and line a 20cm (8in) loose-bottomed flan tin. Refrigerate for 10 minutes, then line with baking paper and baking beans. Cook for 15 minutes, then remove the paper and beans and cook for another 5 minutes or until lightly golden. Cool for 5 minutes.

2 Meanwhile, put the plums or damsons into a saucepan with 4 tablespoons of water and the caster sugar. Cook gently, covered, for 5 minutes or until the fruit is soft. Blend the cornflour with 1 tablespoon of water. Stir into the fruit mixture and cook for 1 minute or until the juices thicken slightly.

3 Place the plums, cut-side up, with any juices in the pastry case. Mix together the nuts, demerara sugar and breadcrumbs and sprinkle over the fruit. Bake for 15 minutes or until the topping is golden.

Served hot with lashings of custard, this pudding is perfect for a cold winter's night. You can make it a day in advance and reheat it, but keep it in the fridge.

DARK CHOCOLATE ICE CREAM

Serves 4

Preparation 10 mins
plus 20 mins cooling and
4 hrs freezing

Cooking 5 mins

Calories 377

Fat 25g

Simplicity

1 Put the milk and sugar in a saucepan and bring to the boil, then quickly stir in the cocoa powder and add the chocolate chunks. Remove from the heat and stir until the chocolate melts. Leave to cool for 20 minutes.

2 Whip the cream until it forms soft peaks. Fold it into the warm chocolate mixture and stir gently until thoroughly combined. Pour into a freezer container and freeze for 4 hours or until firm, whisking the mixture every hour. Serve in scoops, decorated with the mint leaves.

300ml (½ pint) full-fat milk

50g (2oz) soft dark brown sugar

25g (1oz) cocoa powder, sifted

100g (3½oz) plain chocolate, broken into small chunks

142ml carton whipping or double cream

Fresh mint to decorate

Home-made ice creams are delicious, and this is one of the best. You can make it a week or two in advance, but defrost for 20 minutes before serving, to let it soften.

CHOCOLATE BREAD AND BUTTER PUDDING

Simplicity

Serves 4		**Cooking** 40 mins	
Preparation 20 mins		**Calories** 348	
plus 10 mins standing		**Fat** 17g	

15g (½oz) butter

200g (7oz) day-old fruit bread or currant bread, sliced

2 tbsp chocolate and hazelnut spread

2 large eggs

300ml (½ pint) half-fat milk

3 tbsp double cream

1 tbsp sugar (optional)

3 drops vanilla essence

Icing sugar to dust

1 Preheat the oven to 180°C/350°F/Gas Mark 4. Use a little of the butter to grease a 23 x 15cm (9 x 6in) ovenproof baking dish.

2 Cover one side of each bread slice with chocolate spread and cut into triangles if large. Layer the bread, chocolate-side up, in the dish and dot with the remaining butter.

3 Beat the eggs, then beat in the milk, cream, sugar, if using, and vanilla essence. Pour over the bread and leave to stand for 10 minutes before baking. Cook for 35-40 minutes, until well risen and slightly crispy on top. Lightly dust with icing sugar.

If you like bread and butter pudding and you like chocolate, you'll love this. For a change, use panettone – the Italian Christmas bread – instead of fruit bread.

HOT BROWNIES WITH WHITE CHOCOLATE SAUCE

Serves 4

Preparation 20 mins

Cooking 40 mins

Calories 500

Fat 33g

Simplicity

1 Preheat the oven to 180°C/350°F/Gas Mark 4. Grease the sides and base of an 18cm (7in) square cake tin. Beat the margarine and sugar in a bowl until pale and creamy, then beat in the egg, syrup, cocoa powder and flour until it forms a thick, smooth batter. Stir in the nuts.

2 Spoon the mixture into the tin, smooth the top and bake for 35-40 minutes, until well risen and just firm to the touch.

3 Meanwhile, make the sauce. Blend the cornflour with 1 tablespoon of the milk. Heat the rest of the milk in a saucepan, add the cornflour mixture, then gently bring to the boil, stirring as the sauce thickens. Cook gently for 1-2 minutes.

4 Add the white chocolate, then remove from the heat and stir until it melts. Cut the brownies into 8 pieces and serve warm with the chocolate sauce.

100g (3½oz) soft margarine, plus extra for greasing

100g (3½oz) soft dark brown sugar

1 large egg, beaten

1 tbsp golden syrup

1 tbsp cocoa powder, sifted

50g (2oz) wholemeal self-raising flour, sifted

25g (1oz) pecan nuts or walnuts, chopped

For the sauce

1 tbsp cornflour

200ml (7fl oz) full-fat milk

50g (2oz) white chocolate, broken into small chunks

These brownies are delicious when they're cold, but when they're served straight from the oven with white chocolate sauce spooned all over them, they're absolutely fabulous!

Excellent ✓

STICKY CHOCOLATE AND RASPBERRY SLICE

Simplicity

Serves 6

Preparation 25 mins

plus 1 hr cooling

Cooking 30 mins

Calories 298

Fat 19g

75g (3oz) unsalted butter, plus extra for greasing

75g (3oz) plain chocolate, broken into chunks

75g (3oz) fresh or frozen raspberries, defrosted if frozen, plus extra to decorate

2 medium eggs, separated

50g (2oz) caster sugar

25g (1oz) ground almonds

25g (1oz) cocoa powder, sifted

25g (1oz) plain flour, sifted

Icing sugar to dust and fresh mint to decorate

For the sauce

150g (5oz) fresh or frozen raspberries, defrosted if frozen

1 tbsp caster sugar (optional)

1 Preheat the oven to 180°C/350°F/Gas Mark 4. Grease the base and sides of an 18cm (7in) loose-bottomed cake tin and line with baking paper. Melt the chocolate and butter in a bowl set over a saucepan of simmering water, stirring. Cool slightly.

2 Meanwhile, press 75g (3oz) raspberries through a sieve. Whisk the egg yolks and sugar until pale and creamy, then mix in the almonds, cocoa, flour, melted chocolate and sieved raspberries.

3 Whisk the egg whites until they form stiff peaks (this is best done with an electric whisk). Fold a little into the chocolate mixture to loosen, then fold in the remainder. Spoon into the tin and cook for 25 minutes or until risen and just firm. Cool for 1 hour.

4 For the sauce, sieve the raspberries, then stir in the sugar, if using. Remove the cake from the tin and dust with the icing sugar. Serve with the sauce, decorated with mint and raspberries.

This pudding is a real show-stopper. The flavour of the raspberries mingles with the intensely chocolatey cake. Serve with a dollop of crème fraîche or Greek yogurt.

CREAMY CHOCOLATE CHEESECAKE

Serves 8

Preparation 35 mins

plus 20 mins cooling and

2 hrs chilling

Cooking 15 mins

Calories 387

Fat 30g

Simplicity

1 Preheat the oven to 180°C/350°F/Gas Mark 4. Put the biscuits into a plastic bag and crush with a rolling pin. Gently heat the butter and syrup until melted, stirring. Mix in the biscuits, then pack into an 18cm (7in) loose-bottomed cake tin and cook for 15 minutes or until crisp. Cool for 20 minutes.

2 Beat the cream cheese with the sugar until soft. Melt half the chocolate drops in a bowl set over a saucepan of simmering water. Blend the cocoa to a paste with 2 tablespoons of boiling water. Stir it into the melted chocolate and then fold in the cream cheese mixture. Stir in the remaining chocolate drops.

3 Whip 100ml (4fl oz) of the cream until it forms soft peaks. Fold it into the chocolate mixture, then spoon over the biscuit base. Refrigerate for 2 hours or until set. Remove from the tin. Whip the remaining cream and spread over the cheesecake and top with the chocolate shavings.

100g (3½oz) low-fat digestive biscuits

50g (2oz) butter

1 tbsp golden syrup

200g (7oz) cream cheese

2 tbsp caster sugar

100g (3½oz) plain chocolate drops

25g (1oz) cocoa powder, sifted

200ml (7fl oz) whipping or double cream

25g (1oz) plain chocolate, shaved with a vegetable peeler, to decorate

What could be more delicious than a really thick, gooey, chocolatey cheesecake covered in cream? To make it even more decadent, beat a little fruity liqueur into the cream.

HOT CHOCOLATE SOUFFLE

Simplicity

Serves 4

Preparation 20 mins

Cooking 40 mins

Calories 518

Fat 27g

25g (1oz) unsalted butter, plus extra for greasing

150g (5oz) plain chocolate, broken into chunks

6 large eggs, separated

75g (3oz) caster sugar

2 tbsp cornflour

225ml (8fl oz) full-fat milk

Icing sugar to dust

1 Place a baking sheet in the oven and preheat to 200°C/400°F/Gas Mark 6. Lightly butter a 1.5 litre (2¾ pint) soufflé dish. Melt the chocolate with the butter in a bowl placed over a saucepan of simmering water.

2 Whisk the egg yolks and sugar in a large bowl until pale and fluffy. Blend the cornflour with 1 tablespoon of the milk. Heat the remaining milk in a pan, add the cornflour mixture and bring to the boil, stirring. Cook for 1 minute or until thickened. Remove from the heat and stir into the egg mixture with the melted chocolate, combining thoroughly.

3 Whisk the egg whites until they form stiff peaks (this is best done with an electric whisk). Fold a spoonful of egg white into the chocolate mixture to loosen, then gently fold in the rest. Spoon into the dish and place on the heated baking sheet. Cook for 35 minutes or until well risen. Dust with icing sugar and serve straight away.

This soufflé is very light but incredibly chocolatey. People often think soufflés are difficult to make, but once you've had a go, you'll wonder what all the fuss was about.

LEMON AND GINGER SYLLABUB

Serves 4

Preparation 15 mins

plus 30 mins chilling

Calories 396

Fat 34g

Simplicity

1 Whip the cream until slightly thickened. Gradually whisk in the ginger wine or white wine, lemon rind and juice and the sugar.

2 Slice one piece of stem ginger into matchsticks and set aside. Finely chop the remaining piece, then fold into the cream mixture.

3 Spoon the mixture into small glasses or bowls and refrigerate for 30 minutes. Decorate with the reserved stem ginger matchsticks and the mint.

284ml carton double cream

100ml (4fl oz) ginger wine or medium sweet white wine

Finely grated rind and juice of 1 large lemon

50g (2oz) caster sugar

2 pieces stem ginger in syrup, drained

Fresh mint to decorate

Serve this rich lemony pudding with crispy biscuits, such as langues de chats. Don't prepare the syllabub too far in advance, as it may start to separate after a few hours.

LUXURY TIRAMISU

Simplicity

Serves 6

Preparation 20 mins
plus 5 mins soaking and
2 hrs chilling

Calories 519

Fat 37g

12 sponge fingers

150ml (¼ pint) strong
black coffee

150ml (¼ pint) coffee liqueur,
such as Tia Maria

284ml carton double cream

150g (5oz) mascarpone

50g (2oz) caster sugar

50g (2oz) plain chocolate,
grated, plus extra shavings
to decorate

1 Line the base and sides of a 450g (1lb) loaf tin with cling film. Lay 4 sponge fingers in the tin. Mix together the coffee and liqueur and pour one-third of the mixture into the tin. Put the rest of the sponge fingers into a shallow bowl and pour over the remaining coffee mixture.

2 Whip half of the cream until it forms soft peaks. Fold in the mascarpone and sugar. Spread half of the mixture over the sponge fingers in the tin. Sprinkle with 25g (1oz) of grated chocolate.

3 Top with a layer of the soaked sponge fingers, then add the rest of the cream mixture and grated chocolate. Finish with another layer of soaked sponge fingers and refrigerate for 2 hours. Invert the tiramisu onto a plate and remove the cling film. Whip the rest of the cream and spread over the top and sides. Decorate with the chocolate shavings.

You can serve this classic Italian dessert straight away. But it gets even better after it's been in the fridge for an hour or two – as all the flavours soak into the sponge.

HAZELNUT MERINGUES WITH RASPBERRY SORBET

Serves 6

Preparation 25 mins
plus 2-3 hrs freezing and
20 mins cooling

Cooking 1 hr

Calories 284

Fat 19g

Simplicity

1 First make the sorbet. Beat the raspberries with the banana and orange juice, until thoroughly combined. Transfer to a freezer container and freeze for 2-3 hours, stirring once or twice.

2 Preheat the oven to 150°C/300°F/Gas Mark 2. Line 2 baking sheets with baking paper. Prepare the meringue mix according to the packet instructions, whisking until it forms stiff peaks (this is best done with an electric whisk).

3 Fold in the hazelnuts and cornflour. Spoon the mixture onto the baking sheets, making 3 circles on each. Swirl the tops with a fork to flatten, then cook for 1 hour or until crisp. Cool for 20 minutes.

4 Top the meringues with the crème fraîche. Place small balls or curls of the sorbet on top with the raspberries and decorate with the fresh mint.

275g pack meringue mix

50g (2oz) roasted chopped hazelnuts

2 tsp cornflour

200ml carton crème fraîche

100g (3½oz) fresh raspberries

Fresh mint to decorate

For the sorbet

250g (9oz) fresh or frozen raspberries, defrosted if frozen

1 ripe banana, mashed

Juice of 1 orange

The slight tartness of the raspberry sorbet really livens up this beautiful pudding. You can make the sorbet a week in advance, but defrost it for 15 minutes before serving.

UPSIDE-DOWN APPLE TART

Simplicity

Serves 6

Preparation 25 mins
plus 10 mins chilling and
10 mins cooling

Cooking 40 mins

Calories 317

Fat 21g

100g (3½oz) plain flour

1 tbsp cornflour

Pinch of salt

1 tbsp icing sugar

150g (5oz) unsalted butter, softened

50g (2oz) soft light brown sugar

Pinch of ground cinnamon

2 cooking apples, or 4 eating apples, peeled, cored and sliced

---

1 Preheat the oven to 180°C/350°F/Gas Mark 4. Sift the flour with the cornflour, salt and icing sugar, then mix in 100g (3½oz) of the butter until the mixture forms a soft ball. Shape into a round, wrap in cling film and refrigerate for 10 minutes.

2 Place the brown sugar, the remaining butter and the cinnamon in an ovenproof frying pan or 20cm (8in) shallow non-stick cake tin. Heat in the oven for 3 minutes or until the sugar turns syrupy.

3 Arrange the apples in the tin. Roll out the pastry between 2 sheets of baking paper until it is just larger than the pan or tin. Place the pastry on top of the apples, tucking the edge into the inside of the pan or tin. Bake for 35-40 minutes, until the pastry is crisp and golden. Cool for 10 minutes, then invert onto a serving plate.

This twist on a traditional French apple tart, Tarte Tatin, uses a delicious shortbread-style pastry. But if you're in a hurry, use a sheet of ready-made puff pastry instead.

PECAN AND ORANGE TART

Serves 6

Preparation 20 mins
plus 10 mins chilling and
20 mins cooling

Cooking 50 mins

Calories 454

Fat 33g

Simplicity

1 Preheat the oven to 200°C/400°F/Gas Mark 6. Roll the pastry out thinly on a lightly floured surface and use it to line a 20cm (8in) loose-bottomed flan tin. Refrigerate for 10 minutes.

2 Line the pastry with baking paper and baking beans. Cook for 15 minutes, then remove the paper and beans and cook for another 5 minutes or until lightly golden. Cool for 5 minutes.

3 Whisk the egg with the maple syrup or honey, salt, orange rind, sugar and butter until blended. Pour the mixture into the pastry case and arrange the pecan nuts on top. Bake for 30 minutes or until set. Cool in the tin for 15 minutes.

200g (7oz) shortcrust pastry, defrosted if frozen

1 large egg

5 tbsp maple syrup or clear honey

Pinch of salt

1 tsp finely grated orange rind

50g (2oz) caster sugar

50g (2oz) butter, melted

125g (4oz) pecan nuts

This is a fabulous version of pecan pie, but it's still easy to make. It's totally irresistible when served warm from the oven with vanilla ice cream or a little clotted cream.

INDEX